The Comprehensive Interview Guide for Business Systems Analysts

110 Questions and Answers

Sam Oxdell

Welcome to 'The Comprehensive Interview Guide for Business Systems Analysts'. This book is designed as an indispensable resource for aspiring business systems analysts and seasoned professionals alike, offering a wealth of insights, strategies, and practical advice to help you excel in your career and ace your interviews.

Within these pages, you'll find a comprehensive collection of interview questions meticulously crafted to cover a broad spectrum of topics relevant to the role of a business systems analyst. From requirements gathering and process modelling to systems analysis and stakeholder management, each question is carefully designed to assess your knowledge, skills, and expertise across key domains of business analysis.

But this book is more than just a list of questions – it's a valuable tool for honing your interview skills and enhancing your understanding of the business systems analyst role. Alongside each question, you'll find detailed answers and explanations, providing valuable insights into best practices, industry standards, and real-world scenarios.

Whether you're preparing for your first interview or seeking to advance your career to the next level, 'The Comprehensive Interview Guide for Business Systems Analysts' is your trusted companion on the journey to success. Let's dive in and unlock the secrets to mastering the art of business analysis!"

1. **What do you understand by the term 'business systems analysis' and how does it differ from traditional business analysis?**

    - *Answer:* Business systems analysis involves analysing the information systems and technology infrastructure within an organization to improve business processes and achieve strategic objectives. While traditional business analysis focuses on understanding business needs and requirements, business systems analysis delves deeper into how technology can support and enhance those requirements. Business systems analysts bridge the gap between business stakeholders and IT teams, ensuring that technology solutions align with business goals and deliver value.

2. **Can you discuss your experience with gathering and documenting system requirements?**

    - *Answer:* Gathering and documenting system requirements is a crucial aspect of my role as a business systems analyst. I collaborate closely with business stakeholders to elicit their needs and translate them into detailed technical specifications. This involves conducting interviews, workshops, and surveys to gather requirements, and then documenting them using tools such as requirement management software or standardized templates. Clear and comprehensive documentation ensures that all stakeholders have a shared understanding of the system requirements and facilitates effective communication with IT teams.

3. **How do you ensure that system requirements are aligned with organizational goals and objectives?**

    - *Answer:* Aligning system requirements with organizational goals and objectives is essential for the success of any IT project. To ensure alignment, I start by understanding the strategic priorities and business drivers of the organization. I then work closely with business stakeholders to map their requirements to these overarching goals, ensuring that every system requirement contributes directly to achieving desired business outcomes. Regular communication and collaboration with stakeholders help to validate requirements and ensure ongoing alignment with organizational objectives throughout the project lifecycle.

4. **What methodologies or frameworks do you use for system analysis and design?**

    - *Answer:* I have experience with various methodologies and frameworks for system analysis and design, including Agile, Waterfall, and Rational Unified Process (RUP). Each methodology has its strengths and weaknesses, and I adapt my approach based on the specific needs of the project and organizational context. For example, Agile is well-suited for projects with evolving requirements and a need for flexibility, while Waterfall is ideal for projects with well-defined scope and sequential phases.

5. **How do you ensure that system solutions are scalable and adaptable to future business needs?**

    - *Answer:* Scalability and adaptability are critical considerations in system design to ensure that solutions can accommodate future growth and changes in business requirements. To address these concerns, I design systems with modular architectures and flexible components that can easily be scaled or modified as needed. I also conduct thorough risk assessments and feasibility studies to anticipate future business needs and incorporate scalability and adaptability features into the system architecture from the outset.

6. **Can you discuss your experience with data modelling and database design?**

    - *Answer:* Data modelling and database design are essential components of system analysis and design. I have experience with various data modelling techniques, such as entity-relationship modelling and dimensional modelling, to design logical and physical data models that meet the information needs of the organization. I also work closely with database administrators and developers to ensure that database designs are efficient, normalized, and optimized for performance.

7. **How do you approach conducting system testing and quality assurance?**

    - *Answer:* System testing and quality assurance are critical phases in the software development lifecycle to ensure that systems meet functional requirements and quality standards. I develop comprehensive test plans and test cases based on system requirements and acceptance criteria. I conduct various types of testing, including unit testing, integration testing, and user acceptance testing (UAT), to validate system functionality, performance, and usability. Continuous feedback and iteration are essential to identify and address defects early in the development process and ensure that systems meet quality expectations.

8. **What tools and techniques do you use for system analysis and design?**

    - *Answer:* I use a variety of tools and techniques for system analysis and design, depending on the specific requirements of the project. This includes requirements management tools such as IBM Rational DOORS or Microsoft Azure DevOps for documenting and tracking system requirements. I also use modelling tools such as Microsoft Visio or Enterprise Architect for creating system architecture diagrams, data models, and process flows. Additionally, I leverage collaboration tools such as Confluence or SharePoint for sharing documentation and facilitating communication with project stakeholders and team members.

9. **How do you ensure that system solutions are compliant with regulatory requirements and industry standards?**

    - *Answer:* Compliance with regulatory requirements and industry standards is a top priority in system analysis and design, particularly in regulated industries such as healthcare or finance. I conduct thorough research to understand relevant regulations and standards applicable to the project. I work closely with compliance officers, legal counsel, and subject matter experts to ensure that system solutions are designed and implemented in accordance with applicable laws, regulations, and best practices. Regular audits and assessments help to verify compliance and identify areas for improvement.

10. **Can you discuss your experience with system implementation and deployment?**

    - *Answer:* System implementation and deployment involve translating system designs into operational solutions that meet the needs of the organization. I work closely with development teams, system architects, and project managers to oversee the implementation process and ensure that systems are deployed successfully. This includes coordinating system configuration, data migration, user training, and change management activities to minimize disruptions and facilitate user adoption. Post-implementation support and monitoring are also essential to address any issues that arise and ensure that systems continue to meet business requirements.

11. **How do you conduct risk analysis and mitigation planning during system analysis and design?**

    - *Answer:* Risk analysis is an integral part of system analysis and design to identify potential threats and vulnerabilities that could impact system performance or security. I assess risks across various dimensions, including technical, operational, and regulatory, using techniques such as risk matrices or risk registers. I prioritize risks based on their likelihood and impact and develop mitigation strategies to address them. This may involve implementing controls, contingency plans, or risk transfer mechanisms to minimize the impact of identified risks on the project.

12. **Can you discuss your experience with business process automation and workflow optimization?**

    - *Answer:* Business process automation and workflow optimization are key objectives in system analysis and design to streamline operations and improve efficiency. I have experience analysing existing business processes to identify manual tasks and bottlenecks that can be automated or optimized using technology solutions. This may involve implementing workflow automation tools, integrating disparate systems, or redesigning processes to eliminate redundant steps and improve cycle times. The goal is to increase productivity, reduce costs, and enhance the overall customer experience.

13. **How do you ensure that system solutions are aligned with user experience (UX) design principles?**

    - *Answer:* User experience (UX) design principles are essential for ensuring that system solutions are intuitive, user-friendly, and aligned with user expectations. I collaborate closely with UX designers and usability experts to incorporate user-centred design principles into system requirements and interface design. This includes conducting user research, developing personas, and creating wireframes or prototypes to validate design concepts with end users. Iterative testing and feedback loops help to refine the user experience and ensure that system solutions meet usability standards and enhance user satisfaction.

14. **What strategies do you use to facilitate communication and collaboration among cross-functional teams during system analysis and design?**

    - *Answer:* Effective communication and collaboration are critical for success in system analysis and design, particularly when working with cross-functional teams. I employ various strategies to facilitate communication and collaboration, including regular team meetings, status updates, and progress reports. I also use collaboration tools such as Slack or Microsoft Teams to facilitate real-time communication and document sharing. Additionally, I foster a culture of transparency and inclusivity, where team members feel empowered to share ideas, ask questions, and provide feedback openly.

15. **How do you manage competing priorities and deadlines when working on multiple projects simultaneously?**

- *Answer:* Managing competing priorities and deadlines is a common challenge in the role of a business systems analyst, especially when juggling multiple projects simultaneously. I prioritize tasks based on their urgency, importance, and impact on project objectives. This may involve creating a prioritized task list, setting realistic deadlines, and allocating time and resources accordingly. I also communicate proactively with project stakeholders to manage expectations and negotiate timelines where necessary. Time management techniques such as the Eisenhower matrix or Pomodoro technique help me stay organized and focused on key deliverables.

16. Can you discuss your experience with system integration and interface design?

    - *Answer:* System integration and interface design are critical aspects of system analysis and design, particularly in complex IT environments with multiple systems and data sources. I have experience designing and implementing integrations between disparate systems using techniques such as API integration, middleware, or ETL (extract, transform, load) processes. This involves mapping data flows, defining integration points, and ensuring data consistency and integrity across systems. Interface design focuses on creating intuitive user interfaces that facilitate data entry, retrieval, and interaction with the system. I collaborate with UX designers and developers to create interfaces that are user-friendly, responsive, and visually appealing.

17. How do you ensure that system solutions are aligned with best practices and industry standards for software development and IT governance?

    - *Answer:* Aligning system solutions with best practices and industry standards is essential for ensuring quality, reliability, and compliance with regulatory requirements. I stay abreast of industry trends, emerging technologies, and best practices for software development and IT governance through continuous learning and professional development. I adhere to established frameworks and standards such as ITIL (Information Technology Infrastructure Library), COBIT (Control Objectives for Information and Related Technologies), or ISO (International Organization for Standardization) to guide system design and implementation. Regular audits and assessments help to validate adherence to these standards and identify areas for improvement.

18. **How do you approach conducting feasibility studies to assess the viability of proposed system solutions?**

    - *Answer:* Feasibility studies are conducted to assess the technical, economic, and operational feasibility of proposed system solutions before investing time and resources into their development. I analyse factors such as technical requirements, resource availability, cost-benefit analysis, and risk assessment to determine the viability of the proposed solution. This may involve prototyping, proof-of-concept testing, or pilot projects to validate technical feasibility and gather feedback from stakeholders. Feasibility studies help to inform decision-making and ensure that system solutions align with organizational goals and constraints.

19. **Can you discuss your experience with change management and stakeholder engagement during system implementation?**

    - *Answer:* Change management and stakeholder engagement are critical components of system implementation to ensure successful adoption and acceptance of new technology solutions. I develop comprehensive change management plans that address the people, process, and technology aspects of change. This includes assessing stakeholders' readiness for change, communicating the benefits and impacts of the new system, and providing training and support to facilitate user adoption. I also engage stakeholders throughout the implementation process, soliciting feedback, addressing concerns, and celebrating milestones to maintain momentum and support for the project.

20. **How do you measure the success and effectiveness of system solutions post-implementation?**

    - *Answer:* Measuring the success and effectiveness of system solutions post-implementation is essential for continuous improvement and optimization. I define key performance indicators (KPIs) and metrics aligned with project objectives and organizational goals to evaluate

21. **How do you ensure that system solutions comply with data privacy regulations such as GDPR or CCPA?**

    - *Answer:* Ensuring compliance with data privacy regulations requires a thorough understanding of the legal requirements and implications for system design and implementation. I collaborate with legal counsel, compliance officers, and data protection experts to assess the impact of regulations such as GDPR or CCPA on system solutions. This includes implementing data protection measures such as encryption, access controls, and data anonymization to safeguard sensitive information. Regular audits and assessments help to verify compliance and address any gaps or vulnerabilities.

22. **Can you discuss your experience with requirements traceability and impact analysis?**

    - *Answer:* Requirements traceability and impact analysis are essential techniques for managing project scope and identifying dependencies between requirements and other project artifacts. I use tools such as traceability matrices to map requirements to source documents, test cases, and other project deliverables, ensuring that changes are properly tracked and managed throughout the project lifecycle. Impact analysis involves assessing the potential consequences of changes to requirements, such as cost, schedule, and resource implications, and developing mitigation strategies to address them.

23. **How do you ensure that system solutions are aligned with accessibility standards and guidelines for users with disabilities?**

    - *Answer:* Ensuring accessibility is an important aspect of system design to ensure that users with disabilities can access and use the system effectively. I adhere to established accessibility standards and guidelines such as WCAG (Web Content Accessibility Guidelines) to design systems that are inclusive and accessible to all users. This includes providing alternative text for images, ensuring keyboard navigation, and using colour contrast to improve readability. User testing with individuals with disabilities helps to identify and address accessibility issues early in the design process.

24. Can you discuss your experience with business intelligence (BI) and data analytics tools for system analysis and reporting?

- *Answer:* Business intelligence (BI) and data analytics tools play a crucial role in system analysis and reporting by providing insights into organizational performance, trends, and patterns. I have experience using tools such as Tableau, Power BI, or IBM Cognos to analyse data, create visualizations, and generate reports that support decision-making and strategic planning. This involves extracting data from multiple sources, cleansing and transforming data, and developing dashboards or scorecards that provide actionable insights to stakeholders.

25. How do you handle conflicts or disagreements among project stakeholders during system analysis and design?

- *Answer:* Conflict resolution is a common challenge in system analysis and design, particularly when dealing with diverse stakeholders with competing interests. I adopt a collaborative and diplomatic approach to address conflicts, listening to all parties' perspectives and seeking common ground. This may involve facilitating discussions, mediating disputes, or escalating issues to higher management for resolution. Open communication, transparency, and empathy are key to fostering constructive dialogue and reaching consensus on project objectives and requirements.

26. Can you discuss your experience with cloud computing technologies and their implications for system design and architecture?

- *Answer:* Cloud computing technologies offer scalability, flexibility, and cost-efficiency benefits for system design and architecture. I have experience designing and implementing cloud-based solutions using platforms such as Amazon Web Services (AWS),

Microsoft Azure, or Google Cloud Platform. This involves assessing the suitability of cloud services for the project requirements, such as Infrastructure as a Service (IaaS), Platform as a Service (PaaS), or Software as a Service (SaaS), and designing architectures that leverage cloud-native features and capabilities to meet business needs.

27. **How do you ensure that system solutions are resilient and have built-in redundancy to minimize downtime and mitigate risks?**

    - *Answer:* System resilience and redundancy are critical for ensuring high availability and minimizing the impact of disruptions or failures. I design systems with built-in redundancy at multiple levels, such as hardware, network, and data storage, to ensure continuity of operations in the event of failures. This may involve implementing failover mechanisms, load balancing, and data replication strategies to distribute workloads and maintain service levels. Regular testing and disaster recovery planning help to validate system resilience and ensure readiness to respond to unforeseen events.

28. **Can you discuss your experience with system security and risk management practices?**

    - *Answer:* System security and risk management are top priorities in system analysis and design to protect sensitive information and mitigate security threats. I have experience implementing security best practices such as access controls, encryption, and intrusion detection systems to safeguard systems and data from unauthorized access or malicious activities. Risk management involves identifying, assessing, and prioritizing security risks and developing mitigation strategies to address them. This may include conducting security assessments, penetration testing, and vulnerability scanning to identify and address security vulnerabilities proactively.

29. **How do you ensure that system solutions are scalable and can accommodate future growth and expansion?**

- *Answer:* Scalability is essential for ensuring that system solutions can accommodate future growth and expansion without requiring significant redesign or investment. I design systems with scalable architectures and modular components that can be easily scaled up or down based on demand. This may involve implementing horizontal scaling strategies such as load balancing or vertical scaling strategies such as adding more resources or capacity to existing infrastructure. Capacity planning and performance testing help to identify scalability bottlenecks and optimize system designs for future growth.

30. **How do you prioritize system requirements and features to deliver value incrementally and iteratively?**

    - *Answer:* Prioritizing system requirements and features is essential for delivering value incrementally and iteratively, particularly in Agile or iterative development methodologies. I work closely with stakeholders to define and prioritize requirements based on their business value, dependencies, and technical feasibility. This may involve using techniques such as MoSCoW prioritization or user story mapping to identify high-priority features for inclusion in each development iteration. Continuous feedback and validation help to ensure that the most valuable features are delivered early and often to maximize stakeholder satisfaction and project success.

31. **Can you discuss your experience with system performance tuning and optimization?**

    - *Answer:* System performance tuning and optimization are critical for ensuring that systems meet performance requirements and deliver optimal user experience. I have experience identifying performance bottlenecks through profiling, monitoring, and benchmarking tools and implementing optimizations to improve system responsiveness, throughput, and scalability. This may involve optimizing database queries, caching frequently accessed data, or tuning system configurations to maximize resource utilization and minimize latency. Regular performance testing and monitoring help to validate system performance and identify opportunities for further optimization.

32. **How do you ensure that system solutions are aligned with business continuity and disaster recovery requirements?**

    - *Answer:* Business continuity and disaster recovery planning are essential for ensuring that systems remain operational and resilient in the face of unforeseen events or disasters. I collaborate with stakeholders to assess business impact, define recovery objectives, and develop continuity plans that prioritize critical systems and processes. This may involve implementing redundant systems, data backups, and failover mechanisms to minimize downtime and maintain service levels during disruptions. Regular testing and simulation exercises help to validate continuity plans and ensure readiness to respond to emergencies.

33. **Can you discuss your experience with system documentation and knowledge management practices?**

    - *Answer:* System documentation and knowledge management are essential for capturing and sharing valuable information about system designs, configurations, and operations. I have experience creating comprehensive documentation such as system architecture diagrams, technical specifications, and user manuals to provide stakeholders with a clear understanding of system components and functionalities. Knowledge management practices such as wikis, knowledge bases, or document repositories help to centralize and organize information for easy access and reference by project teams and stakeholders.

34. **How do you ensure that system solutions are user-centric and designed with end-user needs in mind?**

    - *Answer:* Designing user-centric system solutions requires a deep understanding of end-user needs, preferences, and behaviours. I conduct user research, interviews, and usability testing to gather insights into user workflows, pain points, and expectations. This informs the design process, allowing me to create intuitive user interfaces, streamline workflows, and prioritize features that enhance user experience. Iterative design and feedback loops help to refine the user interface and ensure that system solutions are user-friendly, accessible, and aligned with end-user expectations.

35. **What strategies do you use to manage dependencies and mitigate risks during system implementation?**

    - *Answer:* Managing dependencies and mitigating risks are critical aspects of system implementation to ensure project success and minimize disruptions. I conduct thorough dependency analysis to identify interdependencies between project tasks, resources, and deliverables, and develop mitigation strategies to address potential risks. This may involve resource allocation, schedule optimization, or contingency planning to minimize the impact of dependencies on project timelines and deliverables. Regular communication and coordination with stakeholders help to manage expectations and proactively address issues as they arise.

36. **Can you discuss your experience with system integration testing and interoperability verification?**

    - *Answer:* System integration testing involves verifying that individual system components work together as intended and interoperability verification ensures seamless communication and data exchange between interconnected systems. I have experience designing and executing integration test cases, defining test scenarios, and validating system interfaces to ensure compatibility and interoperability. This may involve using tools such as API testing frameworks or service virtualization to simulate system interactions and identify integration issues early in the development process. Collaboration with cross-functional teams and third-party vendors helps to coordinate integration testing efforts and address interoperability challenges effectively.

37. **How do you ensure that system solutions are aligned with IT governance and enterprise architecture standards?**

    - *Answer:* Aligning system solutions with IT governance and enterprise architecture standards is essential for ensuring consistency, interoperability, and compliance with organizational policies and guidelines. I adhere to established governance frameworks such as TOGAF (The Open Group Architecture Framework) or Zachman Framework to guide system design and implementation. This includes conducting architecture reviews, assessing adherence to architectural principles, and aligning system solutions with enterprise-wide standards for technology, security, and data management. Regular audits and assessments help to validate compliance with IT governance requirements and identify areas for improvement.

38. **Can you discuss your experience with vendor management and procurement processes for system solutions?**

    - *Answer:* Vendor management and procurement processes are critical for acquiring and implementing third-party system solutions effectively. I have experience evaluating vendor proposals, conducting vendor assessments, and negotiating contracts to ensure alignment with project requirements and budgetary constraints. This involves defining evaluation criteria, conducting vendor evaluations, and selecting vendors based on factors such as technical capabilities, financial stability, and reputation. Post-implementation vendor management includes monitoring vendor performance, enforcing service level agreements (SLAs), and addressing issues or escalations as needed to ensure successful project delivery.

39. **How do you ensure that system solutions are aligned with business architecture and strategic objectives?**

    - *Answer:* Aligning system solutions with business architecture and strategic objectives requires a holistic understanding of the organization's business model, processes, and goals. I collaborate with business stakeholders, enterprise architects, and strategic planners to translate business strategies into actionable system requirements. This involves conducting gap analysis, assessing alignment with business capabilities, and defining roadmaps for system evolution and transformation. Regular reviews and checkpoints help to validate alignment with strategic objectives and ensure that system solutions contribute to achieving desired business outcomes.

40. Can you discuss your experience with system maintenance, upgrades, and retirement planning?

    - *Answer:* System maintenance, upgrades, and retirement planning are ongoing activities to ensure that systems remain reliable, secure, and aligned with evolving business needs. I have experience developing maintenance plans, patch management strategies, and upgrade schedules to keep systems up-to-date and mitigate security vulnerabilities or performance issues. This includes conducting impact assessments, regression testing, and user training to minimize disruptions during system upgrades or migrations. Retirement planning involves decommissioning outdated systems, archiving data, and transitioning users to new platforms or solutions in a seamless manner. Regular audits and performance monitoring help to identify opportunities for system optimization, rationalization, or consolidation to reduce maintenance overhead and support long-term sustainability.

41. How do you approach requirements validation and verification to ensure that they accurately reflect stakeholder needs and expectations?

    - *Answer:* Requirements validation and verification are critical steps to ensure that system solutions meet stakeholder needs and expectations. I use techniques such as requirement reviews, walkthroughs, and inspections to validate requirements against stakeholder feedback and acceptance criteria. This involves engaging stakeholders in the review process, soliciting feedback on requirements documentation, and ensuring that requirements are complete, consistent, and traceable. Verification activities include verifying that requirements are testable, measurable, and aligned with project objectives before proceeding to system design and development.

42. Can you discuss your experience with system modelling and simulation techniques for system analysis and design?

    - *Answer:* System modelling and simulation techniques are valuable tools for visualizing system behaviour, analysing performance, and validating design decisions. I have experience using modelling languages such as UML (Unified Modelling Language) to create system architecture diagrams, sequence diagrams, and state diagrams that capture system structure and behaviour. Simulation techniques such as Monte Carlo analysis or discrete event simulation help to assess system performance under different scenarios and identify potential bottlenecks or areas for improvement. Model-based design facilitates collaboration and communication among project stakeholders and ensures that system designs are well-structured and aligned with project objectives.

43. **How do you ensure that system solutions are aligned with usability standards and design principles for optimal user experience?**

    - *Answer:* Ensuring optimal user experience is essential for the success of system solutions. I adhere to usability standards and design principles such as Nielsen's heuristics or Shneiderman's eight golden rules to create interfaces that are intuitive, efficient, and user-friendly. This includes conducting usability testing, heuristic evaluations, and user surveys to gather feedback on system usability and identify areas for improvement. Iterative design and prototyping help to refine the user interface and ensure that system solutions meet usability standards and enhance user satisfaction.

44. **Can you discuss your experience with system configuration management and version control practices?**

    - *Answer:* System configuration management and version control are essential for managing changes to system configurations, codebases, and project artifacts throughout the development lifecycle. I use version control systems such as Git or SVN to track changes, manage revisions, and coordinate collaborative development efforts among team members. Configuration management practices such as configuration baselining, change control, and release management help to ensure consistency, stability, and traceability of system configurations across environments. Regular audits and inspections help to enforce compliance with configuration management policies and identify opportunities for process improvement.

45. **How do you ensure that system solutions are aligned with IT service management (ITSM) processes and best practices?**
    - *Answer:* Aligning system solutions with IT service management (ITSM) processes is essential for ensuring operational efficiency, service quality, and customer satisfaction. I adhere to ITSM frameworks such as ITIL (Information Technology Infrastructure Library) to guide system design and implementation. This includes defining service management processes such as incident management, problem management, and change management to support system operations and maintenance. Service level agreements (SLAs), key performance indicators (KPIs), and continuous improvement practices help to monitor service delivery and drive ongoing optimization and innovation.

46. **Can you discuss your experience with system performance monitoring and tuning in production environments?**

    - *Answer:* System performance monitoring and tuning are ongoing activities to ensure that systems meet performance objectives and deliver optimal user experience in production environments. I have experience using monitoring tools such as Nagios, Zabbix, or Prometheus to collect performance metrics, analyse system behaviour, and identify performance bottlenecks or anomalies. Performance tuning involves optimizing system configurations, resource utilization, and workload management to improve system responsiveness, throughput, and scalability. This may include adjusting parameters such as memory allocation, disk I/O, or network bandwidth to achieve optimal performance under varying load conditions.

47. **How do you ensure that system solutions are aligned with industry-specific regulations and compliance requirements?**

    - *Answer:* Ensuring compliance with industry-specific regulations and compliance requirements is essential for mitigating legal and financial risks and maintaining stakeholder trust. I conduct thorough research to understand relevant regulations and standards applicable to the industry, such as HIPAA for healthcare or PCI DSS for payment card industry. I collaborate with legal counsel, compliance officers, and subject matter experts to interpret regulatory requirements and translate them into system design and implementation guidelines. Regular audits and assessments help to validate compliance and address any gaps or vulnerabilities proactively.

48. Can you discuss your experience with system migration and data conversion projects?

    - *Answer:* System migration and data conversion projects involve transitioning from legacy systems to new platforms or solutions while preserving data integrity and minimizing disruptions to business operations. I have experience developing migration strategies, data migration plans, and conversion scripts to facilitate seamless migration of data and applications. This includes assessing data quality, mapping data structures, and performing data cleansing and transformation activities to ensure compatibility and consistency between source and target systems. Rigorous testing and validation help to verify migration accuracy and completeness and minimize the risk of data loss or corruption.

49. How do you ensure that system solutions are aligned with scalability requirements and can accommodate future growth and expansion?

    - *Answer:* Ensuring scalability is essential for accommodating future growth and expansion without requiring significant redesign or investment in system solutions. I design systems with scalable architectures and modular components that can be easily scaled up or down based on demand. This may involve implementing horizontal scaling strategies such as load balancing or vertical scaling strategies such as adding more resources or capacity to existing infrastructure. Capacity planning and performance testing help to identify scalability bottlenecks and optimize system designs for future growth while ensuring optimal performance and resource utilization.

50. Can you discuss your experience with system security testing and vulnerability assessment?

    - *Answer:* System security testing and vulnerability assessment are essential for identifying and addressing security vulnerabilities and mitigating risks to system integrity and confidentiality. I have experience conducting security assessments, penetration testing, and vulnerability scanning to identify security weaknesses and assess system resilience against potential threats or attacks. This includes evaluating access controls, encryption mechanisms, and authentication protocols to ensure compliance with security policies and industry standards. Remediation plans and risk mitigation strategies help to address identified vulnerabilities and strengthen system security posture over time.

51. **How do you ensure that system solutions are aligned with user acceptance criteria and deliverables?**

    - *Answer:* Ensuring alignment with user acceptance criteria and deliverables is essential for meeting stakeholder expectations and project objectives. I collaborate closely with stakeholders to define clear acceptance criteria that specify the conditions under which the system will be accepted. This may include functional requirements, performance metrics, usability standards, and regulatory compliance criteria. Regular validation and verification activities help to ensure that system solutions meet acceptance criteria and deliverables before transitioning to production.

52. **Can you discuss your experience with system documentation management and version control practices?**

    - *Answer:* System documentation management and version control are critical for maintaining accurate, up-to-date documentation and ensuring traceability of changes throughout the development lifecycle. I use document management systems such as SharePoint or Confluence to store, organize, and version-control project documentation, including requirements documents, design specifications, and technical manuals. Version control practices such as check-in/check-out, branching, and merging help to track document revisions, manage concurrent edits, and ensure document integrity and consistency across project teams.

53. **How do you ensure that system solutions are aligned with project management methodologies and best practices?**

- *Answer:* Aligning system solutions with project management methodologies and best practices is essential for ensuring project success, stakeholder satisfaction, and timely delivery. I have experience working within various project management frameworks such as Agile, Scrum, or Waterfall, adapting my approach based on project requirements and organizational context. This includes defining project objectives, establishing project plans, and monitoring progress against milestones and deliverables. Regular communication, collaboration, and stakeholder engagement help to manage expectations and mitigate project risks throughout the development lifecycle.

54. **Can you discuss your experience with system deployment and release management practices?**

    - *Answer:* System deployment and release management practices are essential for ensuring smooth, controlled, and efficient rollout of system solutions into production environments. I have experience developing deployment plans, release schedules, and rollback procedures to manage deployment activities and minimize disruption to business operations. This includes coordinating with development teams, system administrators, and stakeholders to execute deployment activities, perform smoke tests, and validate system functionality in production. Change management processes help to track and document changes, manage risks, and ensure compliance with organizational policies and procedures.

55. **How do you approach conducting post-implementation reviews and lessons learned sessions to capture feedback and identify areas for improvement?**

    - *Answer:* Conducting post-implementation reviews and lessons learned sessions is essential for capturing feedback, evaluating project performance, and identifying opportunities for improvement. I schedule post-implementation reviews with project stakeholders to assess project outcomes against success criteria, review project deliverables, and solicit feedback on process effectiveness and stakeholder satisfaction. Lessons learned sessions involve documenting project experiences, identifying best practices, and capturing recommendations for future projects. This continuous improvement process helps to foster a culture of learning, innovation, and excellence within the organization.

56. **Can you discuss your experience with system training and knowledge transfer activities for end users and support staff?**

    - *Answer:* System training and knowledge transfer activities are essential for ensuring successful adoption and effective use of system solutions by end users and support staff. I develop training plans, training materials, and training schedules to facilitate user onboarding, skill development, and proficiency in using system functionalities. This includes conducting instructor-led training sessions, creating e-learning modules, and providing job aids or user guides to support self-directed learning. Knowledge transfer activities involve sharing system documentation, best practices, and troubleshooting tips with support staff to enable them to provide timely assistance and resolve user inquiries or issues.

57. **How do you ensure that system solutions are aligned with enterprise architecture principles and guidelines?**

    - *Answer:* Aligning system solutions with enterprise architecture principles and guidelines is essential for ensuring consistency, interoperability, and scalability across the organization's IT landscape. I collaborate with enterprise architects to define architectural standards, reference models, and design patterns that guide system design and implementation. This includes conducting architecture reviews, assessing adherence to architectural principles, and aligning system solutions with enterprise-wide standards for technology, security, and data management. Regular governance checkpoints help to ensure compliance with enterprise architecture guidelines and facilitate coordination and collaboration among project teams and stakeholders.

58. **Can you discuss your experience with system performance benchmarking and optimization techniques?**

- *Answer:* System performance benchmarking and optimization techniques are essential for assessing system performance, identifying bottlenecks, and improving efficiency and scalability. I have experience conducting performance tests, load tests, and stress tests to measure system response times, throughput, and resource utilization under different workload scenarios. Benchmarking against industry standards or peer organizations helps to establish performance targets and benchmarks for comparison. Optimization techniques such as code profiling, query optimization, and resource tuning help to address performance bottlenecks and improve system responsiveness, reliability, and scalability.

59. How do you ensure that system solutions are aligned with business continuity and disaster recovery plans?

    - *Answer:* Ensuring alignment with business continuity and disaster recovery plans is essential for minimizing downtime, data loss, and business impact in the event of unforeseen events or disasters. I collaborate with business continuity planners, disaster recovery specialists, and IT infrastructure teams to assess system resilience, define recovery objectives, and develop continuity and recovery plans that prioritize critical systems and processes. This includes implementing redundant systems, data backups, and failover mechanisms to ensure continuity of operations and maintain service levels during disruptions.

60. Can you discuss your experience with system governance and compliance monitoring practices?

    - *Answer:* System governance and compliance monitoring practices are essential for ensuring adherence to regulatory requirements, organizational policies, and industry standards. I have experience establishing governance frameworks, control frameworks, and compliance monitoring processes to assess system performance, integrity, and security. This includes conducting regular audits, assessments, and reviews to validate compliance with applicable laws, regulations, and industry standards such as PCI DSS, HIPAA, or SOX. Remediation plans and corrective actions help to address non-compliance issues and mitigate risks to system integrity and confidentiality.

61. How do you approach conducting root cause analysis and problem resolution for system issues and incidents?

    - *Answer:* Conducting root cause analysis and problem resolution for system issues and incidents involves identifying underlying causes, addressing systemic issues, and implementing preventive measures to minimize recurrence. I use techniques such as fishbone diagrams, 5 Whys analysis, or Pareto charts to investigate system failures, performance degradation, or service disruptions. This includes collecting data, analysing logs, and correlating events to identify patterns, trends, and contributing factors. Collaborating with cross-functional teams and subject matter experts helps to diagnose complex issues and develop effective solutions that address root causes and prevent future incidents.

62. Can you discuss your experience with system architecture design patterns and best practices?

    - *Answer:* System architecture design patterns and best practices provide reusable solutions to common design challenges, ensuring scalability, flexibility, and maintainability of system solutions. I have experience applying architectural patterns such as layered architecture, microservices architecture, or event-driven architecture to design systems that are modular, loosely coupled, and highly cohesive. This includes identifying design principles, such as separation of concerns, encapsulation, and abstraction, that guide system design decisions and promote architectural integrity and resilience. Regular architecture reviews and design inspections help to validate adherence to design patterns and identify opportunities for optimization and improvement.

63. How do you ensure that system solutions are aligned with quality assurance and testing standards?

    - *Answer:* Ensuring alignment with quality assurance and testing standards is essential for delivering reliable, high-quality system solutions that meet stakeholder expectations and regulatory requirements. I collaborate with quality assurance specialists, testing engineers, and project stakeholders to define test strategies, test plans, and test cases that verify system functionality, performance, and security. This includes conducting functional testing, regression testing, and penetration testing to validate system requirements and identify defects or vulnerabilities. Test automation, continuous integration, and test-driven development practices help to streamline testing processes and ensure early detection and resolution of issues.

64. **Can you discuss your experience with system architecture evaluation and trade-off analysis?**

    - *Answer:* System architecture evaluation and trade-off analysis involve assessing alternative design options, evaluating trade-offs, and selecting the most appropriate architectural solutions based on project requirements and constraints. I use techniques such as architectural reviews, design inspections, and architectural decision records to evaluate architectural trade-offs such as performance vs. scalability, flexibility vs. complexity, or cost vs. functionality. This includes considering factors such as system requirements, stakeholder preferences, technical feasibility, and organizational priorities to make informed architectural decisions that optimize system performance, maintainability, and cost-effectiveness.

65. **How do you ensure that system solutions are aligned with data governance and information security policies?**

    - *Answer:* Ensuring alignment with data governance and information security policies is essential for protecting sensitive information, ensuring data integrity, and maintaining regulatory compliance. I collaborate with data governance officers, information security specialists, and compliance auditors to define data classification, access controls, and encryption standards that govern data usage and protection. This includes implementing data governance frameworks such as DAMA (Data Management Association) or COBIT (Control Objectives for Information and Related Technologies) to establish data stewardship, data lineage, and data quality management processes. Regular audits, access reviews, and security assessments help to validate compliance with data governance and information security policies and address any gaps or vulnerabilities proactively.

66. Can you discuss your experience with system performance tuning and optimization in cloud environments?

- *Answer:* System performance tuning and optimization in cloud environments involve leveraging cloud-native features and capabilities to improve system responsiveness, scalability, and cost-effectiveness. I have experience designing and implementing cloud-based solutions using platforms such as Amazon Web Services (AWS), Microsoft Azure, or Google Cloud Platform. This includes leveraging auto-scaling, elastic load balancing, and serverless computing services to dynamically adjust resource allocation based on workload demands and optimize system performance and cost efficiency. Cloud monitoring and analytics tools help to identify performance bottlenecks, optimize resource utilization, and improve system reliability and availability.

67. How do you ensure that system solutions are aligned with regulatory requirements for data privacy and protection?

- *Answer:* Ensuring alignment with regulatory requirements for data privacy and protection is essential for mitigating legal and financial risks and maintaining stakeholder trust. I collaborate with legal counsel, compliance officers, and data protection experts to assess the impact of regulations such as GDPR (General Data Protection Regulation) or CCPA (California Consumer Privacy Act) on system solutions. This includes implementing data protection measures such as encryption, access controls, and data anonymization to safeguard sensitive information. Regular audits, privacy impact assessments, and compliance reviews help to validate adherence to regulatory requirements and address any gaps or vulnerabilities proactively.

68. Can you discuss your experience with system disaster recovery planning and testing?

- *Answer:* System disaster recovery planning and testing are essential for ensuring business continuity and minimizing downtime in the event of unforeseen events or disasters. I collaborate with business continuity planners, disaster recovery specialists, and IT infrastructure teams to develop comprehensive disaster recovery plans that prioritize critical systems and processes. This includes identifying recovery objectives, defining recovery time objectives (RTOs) and recovery point objectives (RPOs), and establishing recovery procedures and protocols. Regular disaster recovery drills, tabletop exercises, and simulations help to validate recovery plans, train response teams, and ensure readiness to respond to emergencies.

69. **How do you ensure that system solutions are aligned with industry best practices and standards for software development and IT governance?**

    - *Answer:* Ensuring alignment with industry best practices and standards for software development and IT governance is essential for delivering quality, reliable, and compliant system solutions. I stay abreast of industry trends, emerging technologies, and best practices through continuous learning and professional development. I adhere to established frameworks and standards such as ITIL (Information Technology Infrastructure Library), COBIT (Control Objectives for Information and Related Technologies), or ISO (International Organization for Standardization) to guide system design and implementation. Regular audits, assessments, and compliance checks help to validate adherence to best practices and standards and identify areas for improvement.

70. **Can you discuss your experience with system integration testing and interoperability verification in multi-vendor environments?**

    - *Answer:* System integration testing and interoperability verification in multi-vendor environments involve validating that systems and components from different vendors work together seamlessly and exchange data effectively. I have experience designing and executing integration test cases, defining test scenarios, and conducting interoperability tests to ensure compatibility and interoperability between heterogeneous systems. This includes coordinating with vendors, system integrators, and third-party suppliers to establish communication protocols, data formats, and interoperability standards. Collaboration, communication, and documentation help to manage dependencies, resolve interoperability issues, and ensure successful integration and deployment of system solutions.

71. **How do you approach conducting risk assessments and developing risk mitigation strategies for system projects?**

    - *Answer:* Conducting risk assessments and developing risk mitigation strategies are essential for identifying and addressing potential risks and uncertainties that may impact project success and stakeholder satisfaction. I use techniques such as risk identification, risk analysis, and risk prioritization to assess project risks in terms of likelihood, impact, and urgency. This includes creating risk registers, risk matrices, and risk heat maps to document identified risks and their potential consequences. Risk mitigation strategies such as risk avoidance, risk transfer, or risk acceptance help to manage risks proactively and minimize their impact on project objectives and outcomes.

72. **Can you discuss your experience with system capacity planning and performance forecasting?**

    - *Answer:* System capacity planning and performance forecasting involve estimating future resource requirements and performance needs to ensure that systems can support anticipated workloads and user demands. I have experience analysing historical data, collecting performance metrics, and conducting trend analysis to forecast future demand and capacity utilization. This includes defining capacity planning models, performance indicators, and service level objectives (SLOs) that guide capacity planning decisions and resource allocation strategies. Scalability testing, load testing, and stress testing help to validate capacity plans and ensure that systems can scale to meet growing demand while maintaining optimal performance and availability.

73. **How do you ensure that system solutions are aligned with business process reengineering and optimization initiatives?**

- *Answer:* Ensuring alignment with business process reengineering and optimization initiatives involves identifying opportunities for process improvement, streamlining workflows, and enhancing operational efficiency through technology-enabled solutions. I collaborate with business process analysts, process owners, and subject matter experts to analyse current state processes, identify pain points, and define future state objectives. This includes conducting process mapping, value stream analysis, and gap analysis to identify opportunities for automation, standardization, and optimization. System solutions are designed to support reengineered processes and enable end-to-end workflow automation, reducing cycle times, errors, and costs while improving productivity and customer satisfaction.

74. **Can you discuss your experience with system governance frameworks such as COBIT, ITIL, or TOGAF?**

    - *Answer:* System governance frameworks such as COBIT (Control Objectives for Information and Related Technologies), ITIL (Information Technology Infrastructure Library), or TOGAF (The Open Group Architecture Framework) provide guidelines, best practices, and standards for managing and governing IT systems and services. I have experience applying these frameworks to guide system design, implementation, and operation in alignment with organizational objectives, policies, and regulatory requirements. This includes establishing governance structures, control mechanisms, and performance metrics to ensure accountability, transparency, and compliance with governance principles. Regular audits, assessments, and reviews help to validate adherence to governance frameworks and identify areas for improvement and optimization.

75. **How do you ensure that system solutions are aligned with software development lifecycle (SDLC) methodologies and best practices?**

    - *Answer:* Ensuring alignment with software development lifecycle (SDLC) methodologies and best practices is essential for delivering high-quality, reliable, and maintainable system solutions. I have experience working within various SDLC methodologies such as Waterfall, Agile, or DevOps, adapting my approach based on project requirements and organizational context. This includes defining project objectives, establishing development processes, and implementing quality assurance and testing practices that ensure alignment with SDLC principles and standards. Continuous integration, continuous delivery, and automated testing help to streamline development processes, improve code quality, and accelerate time-to-market while ensuring compliance with SDLC best practices and standards.

76. **Can you discuss your experience with system architecture patterns and reference architectures for designing scalable, flexible, and maintainable systems?**

    - *Answer:* System architecture patterns and reference architectures provide proven solutions to common design challenges, ensuring scalability, flexibility, and maintainability of system solutions. I have experience applying architectural patterns such as layered architecture, microservices architecture, or event-driven architecture to design systems that are modular, loosely coupled, and highly cohesive. This includes leveraging design principles such as separation of concerns, encapsulation, and abstraction to guide system design decisions and promote architectural integrity and resilience. Regular architecture reviews, design inspections, and knowledge sharing sessions help to validate adherence to design patterns and identify opportunities for optimization and improvement.

77. **How do you approach conducting stakeholder analysis and managing stakeholder expectations throughout the project lifecycle?**

    - *Answer:* Conducting stakeholder analysis and managing stakeholder expectations are essential for building trust, fostering collaboration, and ensuring project success. I identify key stakeholders, their interests, and their influence on project outcomes, and develop stakeholder engagement plans that define communication channels, frequency, and content tailored to stakeholder needs and preferences. This includes conducting regular stakeholder meetings, status updates, and feedback sessions to solicit input, address concerns, and manage expectations. Transparency, responsiveness, and empathy help to build positive relationships with stakeholders and ensure alignment with project objectives and outcomes.

78. **Can you discuss your experience with system data migration and transformation projects?**

    - *Answer:* System data migration and transformation projects involve transferring data from legacy systems to new platforms or solutions while preserving data integrity and consistency. I have experience developing data migration plans, data mapping documents, and data conversion scripts to facilitate seamless migration of data and applications. This includes assessing data quality, identifying data dependencies, and performing data cleansing and transformation activities to ensure compatibility and consistency between source and target systems. Rigorous testing and validation help to verify migration accuracy and completeness and minimize the risk of data loss or corruption.

79. **How do you ensure that system solutions are aligned with enterprise risk management (ERM) practices and principles?**

    - *Answer:* Aligning system solutions with enterprise risk management (ERM) practices and principles is essential for identifying, assessing, and mitigating risks that may impact organizational objectives and outcomes. I collaborate with risk management officers, compliance officers, and internal auditors to identify key risks, assess their potential impact and likelihood, and develop risk mitigation strategies that align with organizational risk appetite and tolerance levels. This includes implementing risk management frameworks such as COSO (Committee of Sponsoring Organizations of the Treadway Commission) or ISO 31000 to guide risk identification, analysis, and response activities. Regular risk assessments, scenario planning, and risk reporting help to monitor risk exposure, track mitigation efforts, and ensure alignment with ERM practices and principles.

80. **Can you discuss your experience with system architecture governance and review processes?**

- *Answer:* System architecture governance and review processes are essential for ensuring that system solutions align with architectural standards, principles, and guidelines and meet organizational objectives and requirements. I have experience establishing architecture review boards, design review committees, or architecture governance bodies that oversee system architecture decisions, assess compliance with architectural standards, and provide guidance and recommendations to project teams. This includes conducting architecture reviews, design inspections, and technical assessments to validate architectural decisions, identify risks and issues, and ensure alignment with organizational strategies, policies, and best practices. Regular governance checkpoints and audits help to enforce compliance with architecture governance processes and drive continuous improvement and optimization of system architectures.

81. **How do you ensure that system solutions are aligned with software quality assurance (QA) standards and best practices?**

    - *Answer:* Ensuring alignment with software quality assurance (QA) standards and best practices is essential for delivering reliable, high-quality system solutions that meet stakeholder expectations and regulatory requirements. I collaborate with QA specialists, testing engineers, and project stakeholders to define test strategies, test plans, and test cases that verify system functionality, performance, and security. This includes conducting functional testing, regression testing, and penetration testing to validate system requirements and identify defects or vulnerabilities. Test automation, continuous integration, and test-driven development practices help to streamline testing processes and ensure early detection and resolution of issues. Compliance with software QA standards such as ISO 9001 or IEEE 829 is verified through regular audits, assessments, and reviews.

82. **Can you discuss your experience with system architecture documentation and knowledge management practices?**

    - *Answer:* System architecture documentation and knowledge management practices are essential for capturing and sharing valuable information about system designs, configurations, and operations. I have experience creating comprehensive documentation such as system architecture diagrams, technical specifications, and user manuals to provide stakeholders with a clear understanding of system components and functionalities. Knowledge management practices such as wikis, knowledge bases, or document repositories help to centralize and organize information for easy access and reference by project teams and stakeholders. Regular updates, reviews, and version control mechanisms ensure that documentation remains accurate, up-to-date, and aligned with system architectures and requirements.

83. **How do you ensure that system solutions are aligned with project governance and control processes?**

    - *Answer:* Ensuring alignment with project governance and control processes is essential for managing project scope, schedule, budget, and quality and ensuring project success and stakeholder satisfaction. I adhere to project management frameworks such as PMBOK (Project Management Body of Knowledge) or PRINCE2 (Projects IN Controlled Environments) to guide project planning, execution, monitoring, and control activities. This includes defining project objectives, establishing project plans, and implementing project governance structures, processes, and tools that enable effective decision-making, risk management, and issue resolution. Regular project reviews, status updates, and performance assessments help to monitor project progress, track key performance indicators (KPIs), and ensure alignment with project governance and control processes.

84. **Can you discuss your experience with system architecture modelling and simulation techniques?**

    - *Answer:* System architecture modelling and simulation techniques are valuable tools for visualizing system behaviour, analysing performance, and validating design decisions. I have experience using modelling languages such as UML (Unified Modelling Language) to create system architecture diagrams, sequence diagrams, and state diagrams that capture system structure and behaviour. Simulation techniques such as Monte Carlo analysis or discrete event simulation help to assess system performance under different scenarios and identify potential bottlenecks or areas for improvement. Model-based design facilitates collaboration and communication among project stakeholders and ensures that system designs are well-structured and aligned with project objectives.

85. **How do you approach conducting feasibility studies and technology assessments for system projects?**

    - *Answer:* Conducting feasibility studies and technology assessments is essential for evaluating the viability, benefits, and risks of proposed system projects and selecting the most suitable technologies and solutions to achieve project objectives. I conduct market research, technology scans, and competitor analysis to identify emerging technologies, industry trends, and best practices relevant to the project domain. This includes assessing technical feasibility, economic viability, and organizational readiness through cost-benefit analysis, risk assessment, and stakeholder consultation. Feasibility studies help to inform decision-making, prioritize investments, and mitigate risks by identifying potential challenges, constraints, and dependencies upfront.

86. **Can you discuss your experience with system architecture evolution and transformation initiatives?**

    - *Answer:* System arc improvement and ion and transformation initiatives involve assessing existing architectures, identifying opportunities for improvement, and defining roadmaps for system modernization and transformation to support evolving business needs and technological advancements. I have experience conducting architecture assessments, architecture refactoring, and architecture redesign efforts to enhance system scalability, flexibility, and maintainability. This includes evaluating emerging technologies, architectural patterns, and industry best practices to inform architectural decisions and prioritize transformation initiatives. Collaboration with business stakeholders, technology experts, and enterprise architects helps to align architecture evolution efforts with strategic objectives, drive innovation, and deliver tangible business value.

87. **How do you ensure that system solutions are aligned with data governance principles and best practices?**

    - *Answer:* Ensuring alignment with data governance principles and best practices is essential for managing data assets, ensuring data integrity, and maintaining regulatory compliance. I collaborate with data governance officers, data stewards, and data management professionals to define data governance frameworks, policies, and procedures that govern data usage, access, and protection. This includes establishing data ownership, data classification, and data lifecycle management processes that ensure data quality, consistency, and security across the organization. Regular audits, assessments, and reviews help to validate compliance with data governance principles and identify areas for improvement and optimization.

88. **Can you discuss your experience with system architecture validation and verification techniques?**

    - *Answer:* System architecture validation and verification techniques are essential for ensuring that system designs meet stakeholder requirements, comply with architectural standards, and are fit for purpose. I have experience conducting architecture reviews, design inspections, and technical assessments to validate architectural decisions, identify design flaws, and assess design completeness and consistency. This includes performing architectural modelling, simulation, and prototyping to evaluate system behaviour, performance, and scalability under different scenarios. Stakeholder feedback, peer reviews, and architectural governance processes help to validate architecture quality, identify improvement opportunities, and ensure alignment with project objectives and requirements.

89. **How do you ensure that system solutions are aligned with change management processes and procedures?**

    - *Answer:* Ensuring alignment with change management processes and procedures is essential for managing changes to system configurations, codebases, and project artifacts throughout the development lifecycle. I use change management frameworks such as ITIL (Information Technology Infrastructure Library) or COBIT (Control Objectives for Information and Related Technologies) to define change control processes, assess change impact, and manage change requests in a controlled and systematic manner. This includes conducting change assessments, change approvals, and change implementation activities that ensure changes are implemented with minimal disruption to business operations and mitigate risks to system stability and integrity.

90. Can you discuss your experience with system architecture governance and review processes?

    - *Answer:* System architecture governance and review processes are essential for ensuring that system solutions align with architectural standards, principles, and guidelines and meet organizational objectives and requirements. I have experience establishing architecture review boards, design review committees, or architecture governance bodies that oversee system architecture decisions, assess compliance with architectural standards, and provide guidance and recommendations to project teams. This includes conducting architecture reviews, design inspections, and technical assessments to validate architectural decisions, identify risks and issues, and ensure alignment with organizational strategies, policies, and best practices. Regular governance checkpoints and audits help to enforce compliance with architecture governance processes and drive continuous improvement and optimization of system architectures.

91. How do you ensure that system solutions are aligned with software quality assurance (QA) standards and best practices?
    - *Answer:* Ensuring alignment with software quality assurance (QA) standards and best practices is essential for delivering reliable, high-quality system solutions that meet stakeholder expectations and regulatory requirements. I collaborate with QA specialists, testing engineers, and project stakeholders to define test strategies, test plans, and test cases that verify system functionality, performance, and security. This includes conducting functional testing, regression testing, and penetration testing to

validate system requirements and identify defects or vulnerabilities. Test automation, continuous integration, and test-driven development practices help to streamline testing processes and ensure early detection and resolution of issues. Compliance with software QA standards such as ISO 9001 or IEEE 829 is verified through regular audits, assessments, and reviews.

92. **Can you discuss your experience with system architecture documentation and knowledge management practices?**

    - *Answer:* System architecture documentation and knowledge management practices are essential for capturing and sharing valuable information about system designs, configurations, and operations. I have experience creating comprehensive documentation such as system architecture diagrams, technical specifications, and user manuals to provide stakeholders with a clear understanding of system components and functionalities. Knowledge management practices such as wikis, knowledge bases, or document repositories help to centralize and organize information for easy access and reference by project teams and stakeholders. Regular updates, reviews, and version control mechanisms ensure that documentation remains accurate, up-to-date, and aligned with system architectures and requirements.

93. **How do you ensure that system solutions are aligned with project governance and control processes?**

    - *Answer:* Ensuring alignment with project governance and control processes is essential for managing project scope, schedule, budget, and quality and ensuring project success and stakeholder satisfaction. I adhere to project management frameworks such as PMBOK (Project Management Body of Knowledge) or PRINCE2 (Projects IN Controlled Environments) to guide project planning, execution, monitoring, and control activities. This includes defining project objectives, establishing project plans, and implementing project governance structures, processes, and tools that enable effective decision-making, risk management, and issue resolution. Regular project reviews, status updates, and performance assessments help to monitor project progress, track key performance indicators (KPIs), and ensure alignment with project governance and control processes.

94. **Can you discuss your experience with system architecture modelling and simulation techniques?**

    - *Answer:* System architecture modelling and simulation techniques are valuable tools for visualizing system behaviour, analysing performance, and validating design decisions. I have experience using modelling languages such as UML (Unified Modelling Language) to create system architecture diagrams, sequence diagrams, and state diagrams that capture system structure and behaviour. Simulation techniques such as Monte Carlo analysis or discrete event simulation help to assess system performance under different scenarios and identify potential bottlenecks or areas for improvement. Model-based design facilitates collaboration and communication among project stakeholders and ensures that system designs are well-structured and aligned with project objectives.

95. **Can you discuss your experience with system architecture validation and verification techniques?**

    - *Answer:* System architecture validation and verification techniques are essential for ensuring that system designs meet stakeholder requirements, comply with architectural standards, and are fit for purpose. I have experience conducting architecture reviews, design inspections, and technical assessments to validate architectural decisions, identify design flaws, and assess design completeness and consistency. This includes performing architectural modelling, simulation, and prototyping to evaluate system behaviour, performance, and scalability under different scenarios. Stakeholder feedback, peer reviews, and architectural governance processes help to validate architecture quality, identify improvement opportunities, and ensure alignment with project objectives and requirements.

96. **How do you ensure that system solutions are aligned with change management processes and procedures?**

- *Answer:* Ensuring alignment with change management processes and procedures is essential for managing changes to system configurations, codebases, and project artifacts throughout the development lifecycle. I use change management frameworks such as ITIL (Information Technology Infrastructure Library) or COBIT (Control Objectives for Information and Related Technologies) to define change control processes, assess change impact, and manage change requests in a controlled and systematic manner. This includes conducting change assessments, change approvals, and change implementation activities that ensure changes are implemented with minimal disruption to business operations and mitigate risks to system stability and integrity.
-

97. Question: Can you discuss your experience with system architecture governance and review processes?

Answer: System architecture governance and review processes are essential for ensuring that system solutions align with architectural standards, principles, and guidelines and meet organizational objectives and requirements. I have experience establishing architecture review boards, design review committees, or architecture governance bodies that oversee system architecture decisions, assess compliance with architectural standards, and provide guidance and recommendations to project teams. This includes conducting architecture reviews, design inspections, and technical assessments to validate architectural decisions, identify risks and issues, and ensure alignment with organizational strategies, policies, and best practices. Regular governance checkpoints and audits help to enforce compliance with architecture governance processes and drive continuous improvement and optimization of system architectures.

98. Question: Can you describe a situation where you had to balance technical complexity with business value in a project?

Answer: In a previous project, we had to develop a new feature with complex technical requirements that would significantly enhance the system's capabilities. However, the time and resources required for implementation were substantial, and there were competing priorities and deadlines to consider. I conducted a cost-benefit analysis to evaluate the business value of the feature against the technical complexity and resource constraints. After careful consideration and discussion with stakeholders, we decided to proceed with a simplified version of the feature that delivered the most critical functionality within the available timeframe and resources. By prioritizing business value and managing technical complexity, we were able to achieve our objectives and meet stakeholders' expectations effectively.

99.Question: How do you ensure that technical requirements are aligned with the organization's strategic goals and objectives?

Answer: I start by understanding the organization's strategic goals and objectives, as well as its current and future business needs. I collaborate with stakeholders to identify how technical solutions can support and contribute to these goals. I align technical requirements with the organization's strategic roadmap, ensuring that they are consistent with its vision, mission, and priorities. I also conduct regular reviews and assessments to verify that technical solutions remain aligned with changing business strategies and objectives. By maintaining a strong connection between technical requirements and organizational goals, I ensure that solutions deliver maximum value and impact for the organization.

100.Can you discuss your experience with conducting technical reviews and audits for compliance and quality assurance purposes?

Answer: Conducting technical reviews and audits involves evaluating the design, implementation, and operation of technical solutions to ensure compliance with organizational standards, policies, and best practices. I conduct code reviews, architecture reviews, and configuration audits to assess adherence to coding standards, architectural principles, and configuration guidelines. I identify deviations, deficiencies, and areas for improvement and recommend corrective actions or preventive measures to address them. I also conduct regular quality assurance checks and performance audits to maintain the integrity, reliability, and security of technical solutions and to support continuous improvement and optimization efforts.

101.Question: How do you ensure that technical requirements are aligned with infrastructure and technology considerations?

Answer: Ensuring alignment with infrastructure and technology considerations involves considering hardware, software, network, and cloud services requirements that support the design, deployment, and operation of technical solutions. I collaborate with infrastructure architects, IT operations teams, and technology vendors to define infrastructure requirements, capacity planning, and deployment strategies that meet performance, availability, and scalability requirements. I assess technology options, evaluate vendor solutions, and conduct proof-of-concept trials to select and implement the most suitable technologies for achieving project objectives and delivering value to stakeholders.

102. **Question:** Can you discuss your experience with conducting usability testing and accessibility assessments for technical solutions?

Answer: Conducting usability testing involves evaluating the ease of use, effectiveness, and satisfaction of technical solutions through user interactions and feedback. I design and conduct usability tests, interviews, and surveys to observe user behaviour, identify usability issues, and gather feedback on design and functionality. I analyse test results, prioritize usability issues, and recommend design improvements and enhancements to enhance user experience. I also conduct accessibility assessments to ensure that solutions comply with accessibility standards and regulations, such as WCAG, and provide equitable access to users with disabilities.

103. **How do you ensure that technical requirements are traceable throughout the project lifecycle?**

Answer: I establish traceability links between requirements, design artifacts, and implementation components to ensure alignment and consistency. I use tools such as traceability matrices, version control systems, and requirement management tools to track changes and dependencies. I conduct regular reviews and audits to verify that traceability is maintained and gaps are identified and addressed promptly. I also promote a culture of transparency and accountability, encouraging stakeholders to document and communicate changes to requirements and their associated artifacts. By maintaining traceability throughout the project lifecycle, I ensure that solutions are delivered as intended and meet stakeholders' needs and expectations effectively.

104. Question: What is the purpose of an Entity-Relationship Diagram (ERD), and how do you use it in the context of data modelling?

Answer: An Entity-Relationship Diagram (ERD) is a visual representation of the entities, attributes, relationships, and constraints within a database. It helps to illustrate the logical structure of a database and its various components. I use ERDs during the data modelling phase to identify and define entities, their attributes, and the relationships between them. By visually mapping out the data schema, ERDs facilitate communication and collaboration between stakeholders, including developers, database administrators, and business users, ensuring a common understanding of the data model and its requirements.

105. Question: Can you explain the difference between entities and attributes in the context of data modelling?

Answer: In data modelling, entities represent distinct objects, concepts, or subjects about which data is stored in a database. Attributes, on the other hand, describe the characteristics or properties of entities. Entities are typically nouns, while attributes are adjectives that provide additional information about entities. For example, in a database for a library system, "Book" could be an entity, and attributes associated with it could include "Title," "Author," "ISBN," and "Publication Year."

106. Question: How do you identify and define relationships between entities in an ERD?

Answer: Relationships between entities in an ERD represent the associations or connections between them. I identify relationships by analysing the business requirements and understanding how entities are related or interact with each other. Relationships are classified into different types, such as one-to-one, one-to-many, and many-to-many, based on the cardinality and participation constraints between entities. I use symbols such as lines and crow's feet notation in ERDs to represent relationships and their cardinality, ensuring clarity and accuracy in the data model.

107. Question: What are cardinality and participation constraints in the context of ERDs, and how do you represent them?

Answer: Cardinality and participation constraints define the maximum and minimum number of occurrences of one entity that are associated with a single occurrence of another entity in a relationship. Cardinality refers to the number of instances of one entity that can be related to a single instance of another entity, while participation constraints specify whether the existence of one entity depends on the existence of another entity in the relationship. I represent cardinality and participation constraints using symbols such as "1" (for one-to-one), "N" (for one-to-many or many-to-one), and "M" (for many-to-many) in ERDs, along with optional or mandatory indicators to denote participation constraints.

108. Question: How do you ensure that an ERD accurately captures the data requirements and relationships defined in the business domain?

Answer: To ensure the accuracy of an ERD, I collaborate closely with stakeholders, including business users, subject matter experts, and data architects, to understand and validate the data requirements and relationships defined in the business domain. I conduct requirements elicitation sessions, interviews, and workshops to gather input and feedback from stakeholders, ensuring that the ERD reflects their needs and objectives accurately. I also conduct reviews and validations of the ERD with stakeholders to verify its completeness, correctness, and relevance to the business domain, making adjustments and refinements as needed to ensure alignment with business requirements and expectations.

109. Question: How do you approach conducting gap analyses to identify disparities between current and desired states in technical systems or processes?

Answer: Conducting gap analyses involves comparing current state and desired state to identify discrepancies, deficiencies, and opportunities for improvement in technical systems or processes. As a technical business analyst, I begin by gathering and analysing data, documentation, and stakeholder feedback to establish a baseline understanding of the current state. I then define the desired state based on project objectives, industry best practices, and stakeholder requirements. I identify gaps and discrepancies between the current state and desired state by conducting thorough assessments of processes, systems, capabilities, and performance metrics. I document findings, prioritize gaps based on their impact and urgency, and develop action plans and recommendations to bridge identified gaps and achieve desired outcomes effectively.

110.Question: How do you approach identifying and documenting technical dependencies and interdependencies in complex projects or systems?

Answer: Identifying and documenting technical dependencies and interdependencies is essential for managing risks and ensuring the successful implementation of complex projects or systems. As a technical business analyst, I begin by conducting thorough analyses of project requirements, architecture, and design to identify potential dependencies between components, subsystems, and external systems. I use techniques such as dependency mapping, impact analysis, and interface documentation to visualize and document dependencies effectively. I collaborate with technical architects, developers, and subject matter experts to validate dependencies and assess their impact on project scope, schedule, and resources. I also develop mitigation strategies and contingency plans to address critical dependencies and minimize their potential impact on project delivery and outcomes.

BONUS Question: Can you discuss your experience with conducting technical impact assessments for proposed changes or enhancements to existing systems or processes?

Answer: Conducting technical impact assessments involves evaluating the potential effects of proposed changes or enhancements on existing systems, processes, and infrastructure to identify risks, dependencies, and implications. As a technical business analyst, I collaborate with stakeholders to define the scope and objectives of the proposed changes and assess their technical feasibility and implications. I analyse system architecture, interfaces, and dependencies to identify areas of impact and assess the feasibility, risks, and resource requirements associated with proposed changes. I develop impact assessment reports that summarize findings, recommendations, and mitigation strategies to inform decision-making and guide planning and implementation efforts effectively.

www.ingramcontent.com/pod-product-compliance
Lightning Source LLC
Chambersburg PA
CBHW070950220526
45471CB00007B/2967